ESSENTIAL
Introduction to Computers

and How to Purchase a Personal Computer

OBJECTIVES

**After completing this material,
you will be able to:**

1. Define the term computer and discuss the four basic computer operations: input, processing, output, and storage

2. Define data and information

3. Explain the principal components of the computer and their use

4. Describe the use of magnetic disks, USB flash drives, and other storage media

5. Discuss computer software and explain the difference between system software and application software

6. Identify several types of personal computer application software

7. Discuss computer communications channels and equipment and the Internet and World Wide Web

8. Define e-commerce

9. Explain how to purchase a personal computer

C omputers are everywhere: at work, at school, and at home. In the workplace, employees use computers to create correspondence such as e-mail, memos, and letters; calculate payroll; track inventory; and generate invoices. At school, teachers use computers to assist with classroom instruction. Students complete assignments and do research on computers. At home, people spend hours of leisure time on the computer. They play games, communicate with friends and relatives using e-mail, purchase goods online, chat in chat rooms, listen to music, watch videos and movies, read books and magazines, research genealogy, compose music and videos, retouch photographs, and plan vacations. At work, at school, and at home, computers are helping people do their work faster, more accurately, and in some cases, in ways that previously would not have been possible.

WHAT IS A COMPUTER?

WEB LINK

Computers

For more information, visit scsite.com/ic7/ weblink and then click Computers.

A **computer** is an electronic device, operating under the control of instructions stored in its own memory, that can accept data (input), process the data according to specified rules (process), produce results (output), and store the results (storage) for future use. Generally, the term is used to describe a collection of hardware components that function together as a system. An example of common hardware components that make up a personal computer is shown in Figure 1.

FIGURE 1 Common computer hardware components.

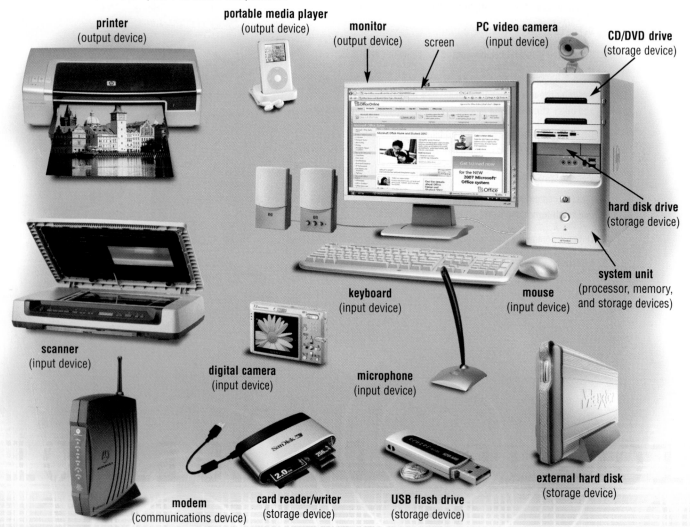

printer
(output device)

portable media player
(output device)

monitor
(output device)   screen

PC video camera
(input device)

CD/DVD drive
(storage device)

hard disk drive
(storage device)

system unit
(processor, memory,
and storage devices)

keyboard
(input device)

mouse
(input device)

scanner
(input device)

digital camera
(input device)

microphone
(input device)

external hard disk
(storage device)

modem
(communications device)

card reader/writer
(storage device)

USB flash drive
(storage device)

WHAT DOES A COMPUTER DO?

WEB LINK

Information

For more information, visit scsite.com/ic7/weblink and then click Information.

Computers perform four basic operations — input, process, output, and storage. These operations comprise the **information processing cycle**. Collectively, these operations change data into information and store it for future use.

All computer processing requires data. **Data** is a collection of unprocessed items, which can include text, numbers, images, audio, and video. Computers manipulate data to create information. **Information** conveys meaning and is useful to one or more people. During the output operation, the information that has been created is put into some form, such as a printed report, or it can be written on computer storage for future use. As shown in Figure 2, a computer processes several data items to produce a grade report.

People who use the computer directly or use the information it provides are called **computer users**, **end users**, or sometimes, just **users**.

DATA

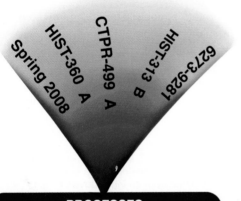

FIGURE 2 A computer processes data into information. In this example, the student identification number, semester, course codes, and course grades all represent data. The computer processes the data to produce the grade report (information).

PROCESSES

- Computes each course's grade points by multiplying the credits earned by the grade value (i.e., 4.0 * 3.0 = 12.00)
- Organizes data
- Sums all credits attempted, credits earned, and grade points (10.00, 10.00, and 36.00)
- Divides total grade points by credits earned to compute term GPA (3.60)

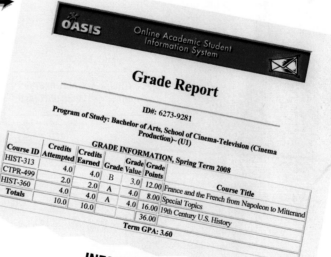

OASIS Online Academic Student Information System

Grade Report

ID#: 6273-9281

Program of Study: Bachelor of Arts, School of Cinema-Television (Cinema Production)– (U1)

GRADE INFORMATION, Spring Term 2008

Course ID	Credits Attempted	Credits Earned	Grade	Grade Value	Grade Points	Course Title
HIST-313	4.0	4.0	B	3.0	12.00	France and the French from Napoleon to Mitterand
CTPR-499	2.0	2.0	A	4.0	8.00	Special Topics
HIST-360	4.0	4.0	A	4.0	16.00	19th Century U.S. History
Totals	10.0	10.0			36.00	

Term GPA: 3.60

INFORMATION

WHY IS A COMPUTER SO POWERFUL?

A computer derives its power from its capability to perform the information processing cycle with amazing speed, reliability (low failure rate), and accuracy; its capacity to store huge amounts of data and information; and its ability to communicate with other computers.

HOW DOES A COMPUTER KNOW WHAT TO DO?

For a computer to perform operations, it must be given a detailed set of instructions that tells it exactly what to do. These instructions are called a **computer program**, or **software**. Before processing for a specific job begins, the computer program corresponding to that job is stored in the computer. Once the program is stored, the computer can begin to operate by executing the program's first instruction. The computer executes one program instruction after another until the job is complete.

WHAT ARE THE COMPONENTS OF A COMPUTER?

To understand how computers process data into information, you need to examine the primary components of the computer. The six primary components of a computer are input devices, the processor (control unit and arithmetic/logic unit), memory, output devices, storage devices, and communications devices. The processor, memory, and storage devices are housed in a box-like case called the **system unit**. Figure 3 shows the flow of data, information, and instructions between the first five components mentioned. The following sections describe these primary components.

FIGURE 3　Most devices connected to the computer communicate with the processor to carry out a task. When a user starts a program, for example, its instructions transfer from a storage device to memory. Data needed by programs enters memory either from an input device or a storage device. The control unit interprets and executes instructions in memory and the ALU performs calculations on the data in memory. Resulting information is stored in memory, from which it can be sent to an output device or a storage device for future access, as needed.

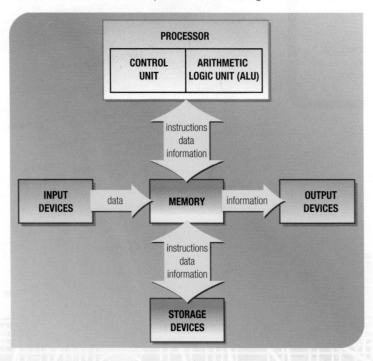

INPUT DEVICES

WEB LINK

Input Devices

For more information, visit scsite.com/ic7/ weblink and then click Input Devices.

An **input device** is any hardware component that allows you to enter data, programs, commands, and user responses into a computer. Depending on your particular application and requirements, the input device you use may vary. Popular input devices include the keyboard, mouse, digital camera, scanner, and microphone. The two primary input devices used are the keyboard and the mouse. This section discusses both of these input devices.

The Keyboard

A **keyboard** is an input device that contains keys you press to enter data into the computer. A desktop computer keyboard (Figure 4) typically has 101 to 105 keys. Keyboards for smaller computers, such as notebooks, contain fewer keys. A computer keyboard includes keys that allow you to type letters of the alphabet, numbers, spaces, punctuation marks, and other symbols such as the dollar sign ($) and asterisk (*). A keyboard also contains other keys that allow you to enter data and instructions into the computer.

FIGURE 4   On a desktop computer keyboard, you type using keys in the typing area and on the numeric keypad.

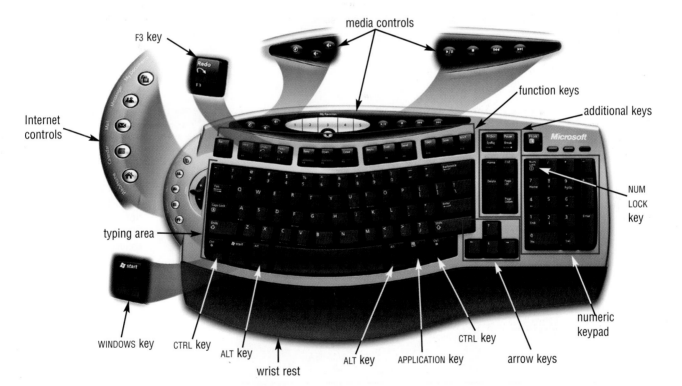

Most handheld computers, such as smart phones, PDAs, and Tablet PCs, use a variety of alternatives for entering data and instructions (Figure 5). One of the more popular handheld computer input devices is the stylus. A **stylus** is a small metal or plastic device that looks like a ballpoint pen, but uses pressure instead of ink to write, draw, or make selections.

Smart phones often include a digital camera so users can send pictures and videos to others (Figure 6).

FIGURE 5 Users enter data and instructions into a PDA using a variety of techniques.

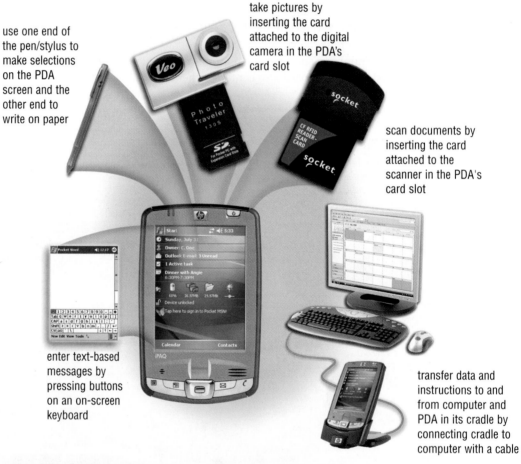

take pictures by inserting the card attached to the digital camera in the PDA's card slot

use one end of the pen/stylus to make selections on the PDA screen and the other end to write on paper

scan documents by inserting the card attached to the scanner in the PDA's card slot

enter text-based messages by pressing buttons on an on-screen keyboard

transfer data and instructions to and from computer and PDA in its cradle by connecting cradle to computer with a cable

FIGURE 6 Many smart phones include a digital camera so users can send pictures and videos to others.

The Mouse

A **mouse** (Figure 7) is a pointing device that fits comfortably under the palm of your hand. With a mouse, you control the movement of the **pointer**, often called the **mouse pointer**, on the screen and make selections from the screen. A mouse has one to five buttons. The bottom of a mouse is flat and contains a mechanism (ball, optical sensor, or laser sensor) that detects movement of the mouse.

Most notebook computers come with a touchpad, a small, flat, rectangular pointing device near the keyboard that allows you to move the pointer by sliding a fingertip on the surface of the pad (Figure 8). Notice in Figure 8 that the notebook computer has the keyboard built into the unit.

FIGURE 7   A laser mouse (a) uses a laser sensor to detect movement of the mouse. It also includes buttons you push with your thumb to navigate forward and backward through Web pages. A media mouse (b) also includes buttons to control media presentations.

(a) laser mouse

(b) optical media mouse

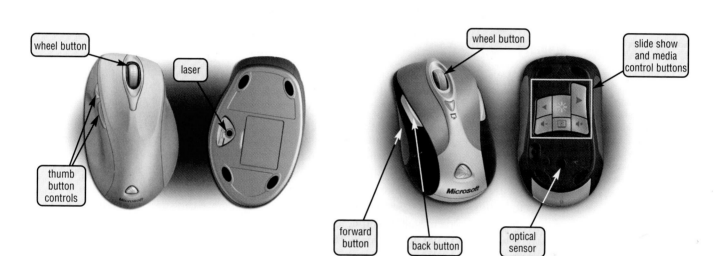

wheel button

laser

thumb button controls

wheel button

slide show and media control buttons

forward button

back button

optical sensor

touchpad

FIGURE 8   Most notebook computers have a touchpad that allows a user to control the movement of the pointer.

SYSTEM UNIT

The **system unit** (Figure 9) is a case that contains electronic components of the computer used to process data. System units are available in a variety of shapes and sizes. The case of the system unit, also called the chassis, is made of metal or plastic and protects the internal electronic parts from damage. The **motherboard**, sometimes called a system board, is the main circuit board of the system unit. Many electronic components attach to the motherboard, such as the processor, memory, and expansion slots. The sound card and video card shown in Figure 9 are examples of adapter cards, which allow a user to enhance the computer system with add-on products.

Processor

The **processor** (bottom right in Figure 9), also called the **central processing unit** (**CPU**), interprets and carries out the basic instructions that operate a computer. The processor is made up of the control unit and arithmetic/ logic unit (Figure 3 on page COM 4). The **control unit** interprets the instructions. The **arithmetic/logic unit** performs the logical and arithmetic processes. High-end processors contain over 200 million transistors and are capable of performing some operations 10 million times in a tenth of a second, or in the time it takes to blink your eye.

Memory

Memory, also called **random access memory**, or **RAM**, consists of electronic components that temporarily store instructions waiting to be executed by the processor, data needed by those instructions, and the results of processed data (information). Memory consists of chips on a memory module (lower left of Figure 9) that fits in a slot on the motherboard in the system unit.

The amount of memory in computers typically is measured in kilobytes, megabytes, or gigabytes. One **kilobyte** (**K or KB**) equals approximately 1,000 memory locations and one **megabyte** (**MB**) equals approximately one million memory locations. One **gigabyte** (**GB**) equals approximately one billion memory locations. A **memory location**, or **byte**, usually stores one character such as the letter A. Therefore, a computer with 512 MB of memory can store approximately 512 million characters. One megabyte can hold approximately 500 letter-size pages of text information and one gigabyte can hold approximately 500,000 letter-size pages of text information.

WEB LINK

Processor

For more information, visit scsite.com/ic7/weblink and then click Processor.

WEB LINK

Memory

For more information, visit scsite.com/ic7/weblink and then click Memory.

FIGURE 9 The system unit on a typical personal computer consists of numerous electronic components, some of which are shown in this figure. The sound card and video card are two types of adapter cards.

OUTPUT DEVICES

Output devices make the information resulting from processing available for use. The output from computers can be presented in many forms, such as a printed report or displaying it on a screen. When a computer is used for processing tasks such as word processing, spreadsheets, or database management, the two output devices more commonly used are the printer and a display device.

Printers

Printers used with computers are impact or nonimpact. An **impact printer** prints by striking an inked ribbon against the paper. One type of impact printer used with personal computers is the dot-matrix printer (Figure 10).

Nonimpact printers, such as ink-jet printers (Figure 11) and laser printers (Figure 12), form characters by means other than striking a ribbon against paper. One advantage of using a nonimpact printer is that it can print higher-quality text and graphics than an impact printer, such as the dot-matrix. Nonimpact printers also do a better job of printing different fonts, are quieter, and can print in color. The popular and affordable ink-jet printer forms a character or graphic by using a nozzle that sprays tiny drops of ink onto the page.

Ink-jet printers produce text and graphics in both black and white and color on a variety of paper types and sizes. Some ink-jet printers, called **photo printers**, produce photo-quality pictures and are ideal for home or small-business use. The speed of an ink-jet printer is measured by the number of pages per minute (ppm) it can print. Most ink-jet printers print from 6 to 33 pages per minute. Graphics and colors print at the slower rate.

A laser printer (Figure 12) is a high-speed, high-quality nonimpact printer that employs copier-machine technology. It converts data from the computer into a beam of light that is focused on a photo-conductor drum, forming the images to be printed. Laser printers can cost from a couple hundred dollars to a few thousand dollars for the home and small office user, to hundreds of thousands of dollars for large business users. Generally, the more expensive the laser printer, the more pages it can print per minute.

FIGURE 10
A dot-matrix printer is capable of handling wide paper and printing multipart forms. It produces printed images when tiny pins strike an inked ribbon.

continuous-form paper

FIGURE 11 Ink-jet printers are a popular type of color printer used in the home. Many photo printers, which can produce photo-lab quality pictures, use ink-jet technology.

FIGURE 12 Laser printers, which are available in both black and white and color, are used with personal computers, as well as larger computers.

color laser printer

WEB LINK

Output Devices

For more information, visit scsite.com/ic7/ weblink and then click Output Devices.

Display Devices

A **display device** is an output device that visually conveys text, graphics, and video information. A **monitor** is a display device that is packaged as a separate unit. Two basic types of monitors are the **flat panel monitor** and CRT. The **LCD monitor**, the most popular type of flat panel monitor, shown on the left in Figure 13, uses a liquid display crystal, similar to a digital watch, to produce images on the screen. Flat panel monitors take up much less desk space and have gained significant popularity over the past few years. The television-like **CRT (cathode ray tube)** monitor is shown on the right in Figure 13. The surface of the screen of either a CRT monitor or LCD monitor is composed of individual picture elements called **pixels**. A screen set to a resolution of 800 x 600 pixels has a total of 480,000 pixels. Each pixel can be illuminated to form parts of a character or graphic shape on the screen.

Mobile computers such as notebook computers and Tablet PCs, and mobile device such as PDAs, portable media players, and smart phones, have built-in LCD screens (Figure 14).

FIGURE 13 The flat-panel LCD monitor (left), and the CRT monitor (right) are used with desktop computers. The LCD monitor is thin, lightweight, and far more popular today than the CRT monitor.

FIGURE 14 Notebook computers, Tablet PCs, ultra personal computers, portable media players, and most PDAs and smart phones have color LCD screens.

ultra personal computer

Tablet PC

notebook computer

portable media player

smart phone

PDA

STORAGE DEVICES

A **storage device** is used to store instructions, data, and information when they are not being used in memory. Four common types of storage devices, sometimes called storage media, are magnetic disks, optical discs, tape, and miniature mobile storage media. Figure 15 shows how different types of storage media and memory compare in terms of relative speeds and uses.

Magnetic Disks

Magnetic disks use magnetic particles to store items such as data, instructions, and information on a disk's surface. Before any data can be read from or written on a magnetic disk, the disk must be formatted. **Formatting** is the process of dividing the disk into tracks and sectors (Figure 16), so the computer can locate the data, instructions, and information on the disk. A **track** is a narrow recording band that forms a full circle on the surface of the disk. The disk's storage locations consist of pie-shaped sections, which break the tracks into small arcs called **sectors**. On a magnetic disk, a sector typically stores up to 512 bytes of data.

Two types of magnetic disks are floppy disks and hard disks. Some are portable, others are not. **Portable storage medium** means you can remove the medium from one computer and carry it to another computer. The following sections discuss specific types of magnetic disks.

FIGURE 15 Comparison of different types of storage media and memory in terms of relative speed and uses. Memory is faster than storage, but is expensive and not practical for all storage requirements. Storage is less expensive but is slower than memory.

		Stores...
Memory	Memory (most RAM)	Items waiting to be interpreted and executed by the processor
Storage	Hard Disk	Operating system, application software, user data and information, including pictures, music, and videos
Storage	Flash Memory Cards and USB Flash Drives	Digital pictures or files to be transported
Storage	CDs and DVDs	Software, backups, movies, music
Storage	Tape	Backups
Storage	Floppy Disk	Small files to be transported

faster transfer rates

slower transfer rates

FIGURE 16 Tracks form circles on the surface of a magnetic disk. The disk's storage locations are divided into pie-shaped sections, which break the tracks into small arcs called sectors.

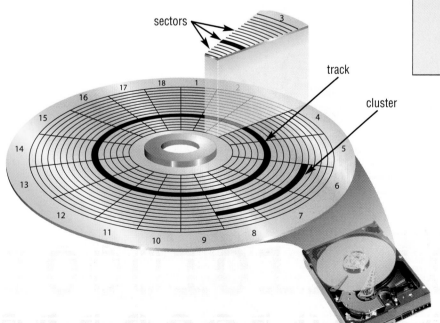

sectors

track

cluster

HARD DISKS A **hard disk**, also called a hard disk drive, is a storage device that contains one or more inflexible, circular platters that magnetically store data, instructions, and information. Home users store documents, spreadsheets, presentations, databases, e-mail messages, Web pages, digital photographs, music, videos, and software on hard disks. The data on hard disks is recorded on a series of tracks located on one or more platters. The tracks are divided into sectors when the disk is formatted. Figure 17 shows how a hard disk works. The hard disk platters spin at a high rate of speed, typically 5,400 to 15,000 revolutions per minute. When reading data from the disk, the read head senses the magnetic spots that are recorded on the disk along the various tracks and transfers that data to memory. When writing, the data is transferred from memory and is stored as magnetic spots on the tracks on the recording surface of one or more of the disk platters.

When reading or writing, the read/write heads on a hard disk drive do not actually touch the surface of the disk. The distance between the read/write heads and the platters is about two millionths of one inch. This close clearance means that dirt, dust, smoke, or other particles could cause a **head crash**, when a read/write head touches a platter, usually resulting in loss of data or sometimes the entire drive. Although current hard disks are sealed tightly to keep out contaminants, head crashes do occasionally occur. Thus, it is crucial that you back up your hard disk regularly. A **backup** is a duplicate of a file, program, or disk that you can use in case the original is lost, damaged, or destroyed.

The number of platters permanently mounted on the spindle of a hard disk varies. On most drives, each surface of the platter can be used to store data. Thus, if a hard disk drive uses one

FIGURE 17 How a hard disk works.

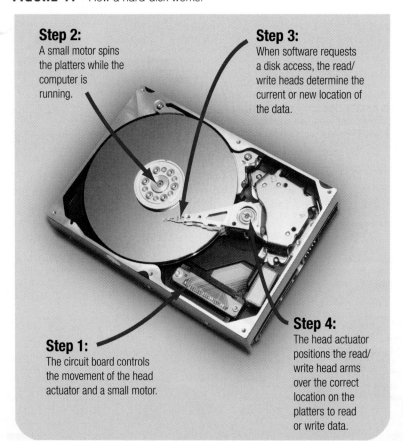

Step 2:
A small motor spins the platters while the computer is running.

Step 3:
When software requests a disk access, the read/write heads determine the current or new location of the data.

Step 1:
The circuit board controls the movement of the head actuator and a small motor.

Step 4:
The head actuator positions the read/write head arms over the correct location on the platters to read or write data.

platter, two surfaces are available for data. If the drive uses two platters, four sets of read/write heads read and record data from the four surfaces. Storage capacities of internally mounted fixed disks for personal computers range from 10 GB to more than 750 GB.

The system unit on most desktop and notebook computers contains at least one hard disk. Although hard disks are available in removable cartridge form, most hard disks cannot be removed from the computer.

FLOPPY DISKS   Another older form of magnetic storage is the **floppy disk**, or **diskette**, an inexpensive portable storage medium (Figure 18a). The most widely used floppy disk is 3.5 inches wide and typically can store up to 1.44 megabytes of data, or 1,474,560 characters. Although the exterior of the 3.5-inch disk is not floppy, users still refer to them as floppy disks. Floppy disks are not as widely used as they were 15 years ago because of their low storage capacity.

A **floppy disk drive** is a device that can read from and write on a floppy disk. Floppy disk drives are either built into the system unit (Figure 18a) or are external to the system unit and connected to the computer via a cable (Figure 18b).

Data stored on a floppy disk must be retrieved and placed into memory to be processed. The time required to access and retrieve data is called the **access time**. The access time for floppy disks varies from about 175 milliseconds to approximately 300 milliseconds (one millisecond equals 1/1000 of a second). On average, data stored in a single sector on a floppy disk can be retrieved in approximately 1/15 to 1/3 of a second.

FIGURE 18   On a personal computer, you insert and remove a floppy disk from a floppy disk drive.

(a) Floppy disk drive installed inside a desktop computer

(b) External floppy disk drive attached to computer with a cable

Optical Discs

An optical disc is a portable storage medium that consists of a flat, round, portable disc made of metal, plastic, and lacquer that is written and read by a laser. Optical discs used in personal computers are 4.75 inches in diameter and less than 1/20 of an inch thick. Nearly every personal computer today has some type of optical disc drive installed in a drive bay. On these drives, you push a button to slide the tray out, insert the disc, and then push the same button to close the tray (Figure 19).

Many different formats of optical discs exist today. These include CD-ROM, CD-R, CD-RW, DVD-ROM, DVD-R, DVD+R, DVD-RW, DVD+RW, and DVD+RAM. Figure 21 on the next page identifies each of these optical disc formats and specifies whether a user can read from the disc, write on the disc, and/or erase the disc.

A **CD-ROM** (compact disc read-only memory) is a type of optical disc that users can read but not write on (record) or erase — hence, the name read-only. A typical CD-ROM holds from 650 MB to 1 GB of data, instructions, and information. Software manufacturers often distribute their programs using CD-ROMs.

To read a CD-ROM, insert the disc in a **CD-ROM drive** or a CD-ROM player. Because audio CDs and CD-ROMs use the same laser technology, you may be able to use a CD-ROM drive to listen to an audio CD while working on the computer. Some music companies, however, configure their CDs so the music will not play on a computer. They do this to protect themselves from customers illegally copying and sharing the music.

Push the button to slide out the tray.

Insert the disc, label side up.

Push the same button to close the tray.

FIGURE 19 On optical disc drives, you push a button to slide out a tray, insert the disc, and then push the same button to close the tray.

A **CD-R** (compact disc-recordable) is an optical disc onto which you can record your own items such as text, graphics, and audio. With a CD-R, you can write on part of the disc at one time and another part at a later time. Once you have recorded the CD-R, you can read from it as many times as you wish. You can write on each part only one time, and you cannot erase the disc's contents. Most CD-ROM drives can read a CD-R.

A **CD-RW** (compact disc-rewriteable) is an erasable optical disc you can write on multiple times. A CD-RW overcomes the major disadvantage of CD-R discs, which is that you can write on them only once. With CD-RWs, the disc acts like a floppy or hard disk, allowing you to write and rewrite data, instructions, and information onto it multiple times.

Although CDs have large storage capacities, even a CD cannot hold many of today's complex programs. Some software, for example, is sold on five or more CDs. To meet these tremendous storage requirements, some software companies have moved from CDs to the larger DVDs — a technology that can be used to store large amounts of text and even videos (Figure 20).

FIGURE 20 A DVD is an extremely high-capacity optical disc.

DVD

DVD drive

OPTICAL DISC FORMATS

Optical Disc	Read	Write	Erase
CD-ROM	Y	N	N
CD-R	Y	Y	N
CD-RW	Y	Y	Y
DVD-ROM BD-ROM HD DVD-ROM	Y	N	N
DVD-R DVD+R BD-R HD DVD-R	Y	Y	N
DVD-RW DVD+RW DVD+RAM BD-RE HD DVD-RW	Y	Y	Y

FIGURE 21 Manufacturers sell CD-ROM and DVD-ROM media prerecorded (written) with audio, video, and software. Users cannot change the contents of these discs. Users, however, can purchase the other formats of CDs and DVDs as blank media and record (write) their own data, instructions, and information on these discs.

A **DVD-ROM** (digital versatile disk-read-only memory) is a very high-capacity optical disc capable of storing from 4.7 GB to 17 GB — more than enough to hold a telephone book containing every resident in the United States. As with the CD-ROM format, you cannot write on an optical disc that uses the DVD-ROM format. You can only read from it. To read a DVD-ROM, you need a **DVD-ROM drive**. Most DVD-ROM drives can also read CDs.

DVD-R and **DVD+R** are competing DVD-recordable formats, each with up to 4.7 GB storage capacity. Both allow users to write on the disc once and read (play) it many times. Two newer, more expensive DVD-recordable formats are **Blu-ray (BD-ROM)** and **HD DVD**, with higher quality and more capacity than standard DVDs. **DVD-RW**, **DVD+RW**, and **DVD+RAM** are competing DVD formats, each with storage capacities up to 4.7 GB per side, that allow users to erase and write (record) many times. **BD-RE** and **HD DVD-RW** are competing higher-capacity rewriteable DVD formats. To write to a DVD, you need a recordable or rewriteable DVD-ROM drive.

Tape

Tape is a magnetically coated ribbon of plastic housed in a tape cartridge (Figure 22) capable of storing large amounts of data and information at a low cost. A **tape drive** is used to read from and write on a tape. Tape is primarily used for long-term storage and backup.

Miniature Mobile Storage Media

Miniature mobile storage media are rewriteable media usually in the form of a flash memory card, USB flash drive, or a smart card. Miniature mobile storage media allow mobile users to transport digital images, music, or documents easily to and from computers and other devices (Figure 23).

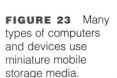

FIGURE 22   A tape drive and a tape cartridge.

FIGURE 23   Many types of computers and devices use miniature mobile storage media.

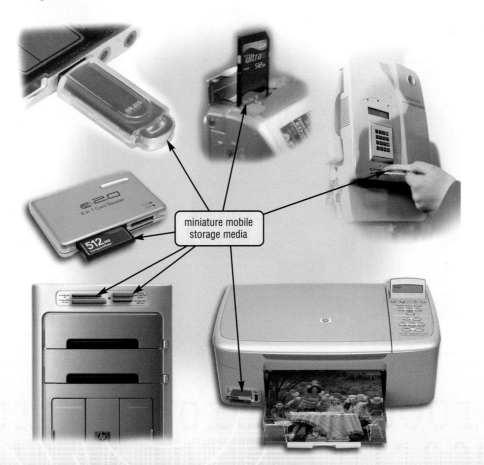

miniature mobile storage media

Flash memory cards are solid-state media, which means they consist entirely of electronics (chips, wires, etc.) and contain no moving parts. Common types of flash memory include CompactFlash (CF), Secure Digital (SD), xD Picture Card, and Memory Stick (Figure 24).

A **USB flash drive** (Figure 25), sometimes called a pen drive or thumb drive, is a flash memory storage device that plugs into a USB port on a computer or mobile device. USB flash drives are the portable storage media of choice among users today, making the floppy disk nearly obsolete, because they are small, lightweight, and have such large storage capacities. Capacities typically range from 32 MB to 64 GB.

VARIOUS FLASH MEMORY CARDS

Media Name	Storage Capacity	Use
CompactFlash	64 MB to 16 GB	Digital cameras, PDAs, smart phones, photo printers, portable media players, notebook computers, desktop computers
Secure Digital	64 MB to 4 GB	Digital cameras, digital video cameras, PDAs, smart phones, photo printers, portable media players
xD Picture Card	64 MB to 2 GB	Digital cameras, photo printers
Memory Stick	256 MB to 4 GB	Digital cameras, digital video cameras, PDAs, photo printers, smart phones, handheld game consoles, notebook computers
Memory Stick PRO Duo	128 MB to 4 GB	Digital cameras, smart phones, handheld game consoles

FIGURE 24
A variety of flash memory cards.

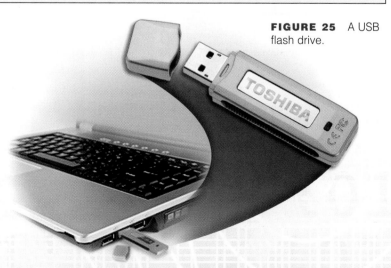

FIGURE 25 A USB flash drive.

A **smart card**, which is similar in size to a credit card or ATM card, stores data on a thin microprocessor embedded in the card. When you insert the smart card in a specialized card reader, the information on the card is read and, if necessary, updated (Figure 26). Uses of smart cards include storing medical records, tracking customer purchases, storing a prepaid amount of money, and authenticating users, such as for Internet purchases.

COMMUNICATIONS DEVICES

A **communications device** is a hardware component that enables a computer to send (transmit) and receive data, instructions, and information to and from one or more computers. A widely used communications device is the telephone or cable modem (Figure 1 on page COM 2).

Communications occur over **transmission media** such as telephone lines, cables, cellular radio networks, and satellites. Some transmission media, such as satellites and cellular radio networks, are **wireless**, which means they have no physical lines or wires. People around the world use computers and communications devices to communicate with each other using one or more transmission media.

COMPUTER SOFTWARE

Computer software is the key to productive use of computers. With the correct software, a computer can become a valuable tool. Software can be categorized into two types: system software and application software.

WEB LINK

Operating Systems

For more information, visit scsite.com/ic7/ weblink and then click Operating Systems.

System Software

System software consists of programs to control the operations of computer equipment. An important part of system software is a set of programs called the operating system. Instructions in the **operating system** tell the computer how to perform the functions of loading, storing, and executing an application program and how to transfer data. For a computer to operate, an operating system must be stored in the computer's memory. When a computer is turned on, the operating system is loaded into the computer's memory from auxiliary storage. This process is called **booting**.

Today, most computers use an operating system that has a **graphical user interface** (**GUI**) that provides visual cues such as icon symbols to help the user. Each **icon** represents an application such as word processing, or a file or document where data is stored. Microsoft Windows Vista (Figure 27) and Windows XP, Apple Mac OS X, and Linux are four popular personal computer operating systems.

FIGURE 26 A smart card and smart card reader.

FIGURE 27 A graphical user interface, such as Microsoft Windows Vista, makes the computer easier to use.

Application Software

Application software consists of programs designed to make users more productive and/or assist them with personal tasks. Some widely used application software includes Web browsers, personal information managers, project management, accounting, computer-aided design, desktop publishing, paint/image editing, audio and video editing, multimedia authoring, Web page authoring, personal finance, legal, tax preparation, home design/landscaping, educational, reference, and entertainment (games, simulations, etc.). Often, application software is available for purchase from a Web site or store that sells computer products (Figure 28).

Personal computer users regularly use application software. Some of the more commonly used applications are word processing, electronic spreadsheet, database, and presentation graphics.

WORD PROCESSING   **Word processing software** (Figure 29) is used to create, edit, format, and print documents. A key advantage of word processing software is that users easily can make changes in documents, such as correcting spelling; changing margins; and adding, deleting, or relocating entire paragraphs. These changes would be difficult and time consuming to make using manual methods such as a typewriter. With a word processor, documents can be printed quickly and accurately and easily stored on a disk for future use. Word processing software is oriented toward working with text, but word processing packages also support features that enable users to manipulate numeric data and utilize graphics.

SPREADSHEET   **Electronic spreadsheet software** (Figure 30) allows the user to add, subtract, and perform user-defined calculations on rows and columns of numbers. These numbers can be changed, and the spreadsheet quickly recalculates the new results. Electronic spreadsheet software eliminates the tedious recalculations required with manual methods. Spreadsheet information frequently is converted into a graphic form, such as charts. Graphics capabilities now are included in most spreadsheet packages.

FIGURE 28   Stores that sell computer products have shelves stocked with software for sale.

FIGURE 29   Word processing software is used to create letters, memos, newsletters, and other documents.

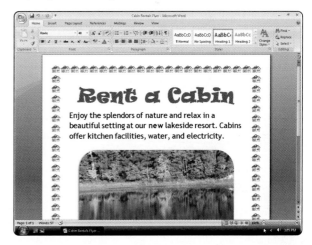

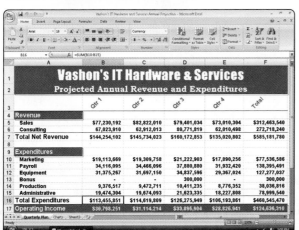

FIGURE 30   Electronic spreadsheet software frequently is used by people who work with numbers. The user enters the data and the formulas to be used on the data, and the computer calculates the results.

DATABASE   **Database software** (Figure 31) allows the user to enter, retrieve, and update data in an organized and efficient manner. These software packages have flexible inquiry and reporting capabilities that let users access the data in different ways and create custom reports that include some or all of the information in the database.

PRESENTATION GRAPHICS   **Presentation graphics software** (Figure 32) allows the user to create slides for use in a presentation to a group. Using special projection devices, the slides are projected directly from the computer.

NETWORKS AND THE INTERNET

A **network** is a collection of computers and devices connected together, often wirelessly, via communications devices and transmission media. When a computer connects to a network, it is **online**.

Networks allow users to share resources, such as hardware, software, data, and information. Sharing resources saves time and money. For example, instead of purchasing one printer for every computer in a company, the firm can connect a single printer and all computers via a network (Figure 33); the network enables all of the computers to access the same printer.

Most business computers are networked together. These networks can be relatively small or quite extensive. A network that connects computers in a limited geographic area, such as a school computer laboratory, office, or group of buildings, is called a **local area network** (**LAN**). A network that covers a large geographical area, such as one that connects the district offices of a national corporation, is called a **wide area network** (**WAN**) (Figure 34).

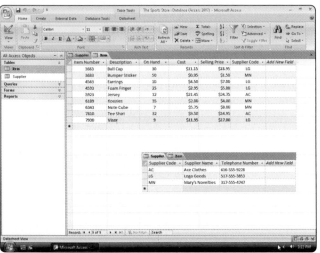

FIGURE 31   Database software allows the user to enter, retrieve, and update data in an organized and efficient manner.

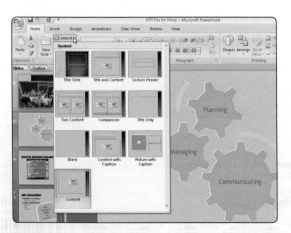

FIGURE 32   Presentation graphics software allows the user to produce professional-looking presentations.

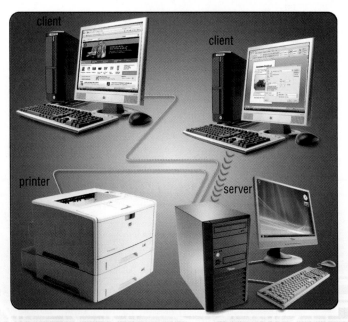

FIGURE 33   The local area network (LAN) enables two or more separate computers to share the same printer.

The Internet

The world's largest network is the **Internet**, which is a worldwide collection of networks that connects millions of businesses, government agencies, educational institutions, and individuals. With an abundance of resources and data accessible via the Internet, more than 1 billion people around the world use the Internet for a variety of reasons, including the following:

- Communicating with and meeting other people
- Accessing a wealth of information, news, and research findings
- Shopping for goods and services
- Banking and investing
- Accessing sources of entertainment and leisure, such as online games, music, videos, books and magazines

Most users connect to the Internet through a regional or national ISP, an online service provider, or a wireless Internet service provider. An **ISP** (**Internet service provider**) is an organization, such as a cable company or telephone company, that supplies connections to the Internet for a monthly fee. Earthlink and AT&T Worldnet are examples of national ISPs. Like an ISP, an **online service provider** (**OSP**) provides access to the Internet, but it also provides a variety of other specialized content and services such as news, weather, financial data, e-mail, games, and more. Two popular online services are America Online (AOL) and The Microsoft Network (MSN). A **wireless Internet service provider** (WISP) is a company that provides wireless Internet access to computers and mobile devices such as smart phones and PDAs. Boingo Wireless and Cingular Wireless are examples of WISPs.

WEB LINK

World Wide Web

For more information, visit scsite.com/ic7/ weblink and then click World Wide Web.

The World Wide Web

One of the more popular segments of the Internet is the **World Wide Web**, also called the **Web**, which contains billions of documents called Web pages. A **Web page** can contain text, graphics, audio, and video, and has built-in connections, or links, to other Web documents. Figure 35 on the next page shows different types of Web pages found on the World Wide Web today. Web pages are stored on computers throughout the world. A **Web site** is a related collection of Web pages. Visitors to a Web site access and view Web pages using a software program called a **Web browser**. A Web page has a unique address, called a **Uniform Resource Locator** (**URL**).

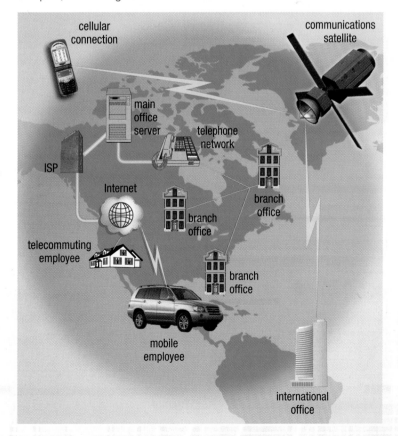

FIGURE 34 A wide area network (WAN) can be quite large and complex, connecting users in district offices around the world.

FIGURE 35 Types of Web sites.

As shown in Figure 36, a URL consists of a protocol, a domain name, sometimes the path to a specific Web page or location in a Web page, and the Web page name. Most Web page URLs begin with **http://**, which stands for **hypertext transfer protocol**, the communications standard used to transfer pages on the Web. The domain name identifies the Web site, which is stored on a Web server. A **Web server** is a computer that delivers (serves) requested Web pages.

Electronic Commerce

When you conduct business activities online, you are participating in electronic commerce, also known as **e-commerce**. Some people use the term m-commerce (mobile commerce) to identify e-commerce that uses mobile devices. These commercial activities include shopping, investing, and any other venture that represents a business transaction. Today, three types of e-commerce exist. **Business to consumer** (B2C) involves the sale of goods to the general public. **Consumer to consumer** (C2C) involves one consumer selling directly to another. **Business to business** (B2B) provides goods and services to other businesses.

WEB LINK

E-Commerce

For more information, visit scsite.com/ic7/ weblink and then click E-Commerce.

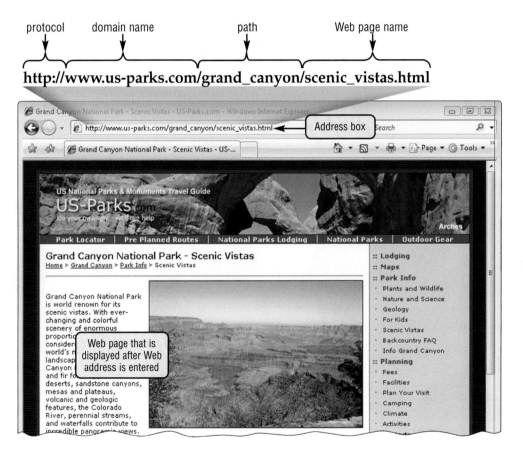

| protocol | domain name | path | Web page name |

http://www.us-parks.com/grand_canyon/scenic_vistas.html

FIGURE 36   After entering the Web address http://www.us-parks.com/grand_canyon/scenic_vistas.html in the Address box, this Web page at the US National Parks Travel Guide Web site is displayed.

How to Purchase a Personal Computer

(a) desktop computer

(b) mobile computer (notebook computer or Tablet PC)

A At some point, perhaps while you are taking this course, you may decide to buy a personal computer. The decision is an important one and will require an investment of both time and money. Like many buyers, you may have little computer experience and find yourself unsure of how to proceed. You can get started by talking to your friends, coworkers, and instructors about their computers. What type of computers did they buy? Why? For what purposes do they use their computers? You also should answer the following three questions to help narrow your choices to a specific computer type, before reading this guide. At the end of this guide, you'll also find tips on purchasing PDAs, smart phones, portable media players, and other personal mobile devices such as handheld navigation devices and game consoles.

1 **Do you want a desktop computer or mobile computer?**
A desktop computer (Figure 37a) is designed as a stationary device that sits on or below a desk or table in a location such as a home, office, or dormitory room. A desktop computer must be plugged in an electrical outlet to operate. A mobile computer, such as a notebook computer or Tablet PC (Figure 37b), is smaller than a desktop computer, more portable, and has a battery that allows you to operate it for a period without an electrical outlet.

Desktop computers are a good option if you work mostly in one place and have plenty of space in your work area. Desktop computers generally give you more performance for your money.

Increasingly, more corporations are buying mobile computers to take advantage of their portability to work while traveling and at home. The past disadvantages of mobile computers, such as lower processor speeds, poor-quality monitors, weight, short battery life, and significantly higher prices, have all but disappeared. Today, hard drive speed, capacity, processor speed, and graphics capability in notebook computers are equal to, if not better than, desktop computers.

If you are thinking of using a mobile computer to take notes in class or in business meetings, then consider a Tablet PC with handwriting and drawing capabilities. Typically, note-taking involves writing text notes and drawing charts,

Should I buy a desktop or mobile computer or personal mobile device?

For what purposes will I use the computer?

Should the computer I buy be compatible with the computers at school or work?

FIGURE 37

schematics, and other illustrations. By allowing you to write and draw directly on the screen with a digital pen, a Tablet PC eliminates the distracting sound of the notebook keyboard tapping and allows you to capture drawings. Some notebook computers can convert to Tablet PCs.

Mobile computers used to have several drawbacks, including the lack of high-end capabilities. Today's high-end notebook computers include most of the capabilities of a good desktop computer. Manufacturers have made great strides in improving durability and battery life. Most notebook computers are 1.5 to 2 inches thick and weigh less than 10 pounds, making them very portable and easy to carry.

2 For what purposes will you use the computer?
Having a general idea of the purposes for which you want to use your computer will help you decide on the type of computer to buy. At this point in your research, it is not necessary to know the exact application software titles or version numbers you might want to use. Knowing that you plan to use the computer primarily to create word processing, spreadsheet, database, and presentation documents, however, will point you in the direction of a desktop or notebook computer. If you want the portability of a smart phone or PDA, but you need more computing power, then a Tablet PC may be the best alternative. You also must consider that some application software runs only on a Mac, while others run only on a PC with the Windows operating system. Still other software may run only on a PC running the UNIX or Linux operating system.

3 Should the computer be compatible with the computers at school or work?
If you plan to bring work home, telecommute, or take distance education courses, then you should purchase a computer that is compatible with those at school or work.

Compatibility is primarily a software issue. If your computer runs the same operating system version, such as Microsoft Windows Vista, and the same application software, such as Microsoft Office, then your computer will be able to read documents created at school or work and vice versa. Incompatible hardware can become an issue if you plan to connect directly to a school or office network using a cable or wireless technology. You usually can obtain the minimum system requirements from the Information Technology department at your school or workplace.

After evaluating the answers to these three questions, you should have a general idea of how you plan to use your computer and the type of computer you want to buy. Once you have decided on the type of computer you want, you can follow the guidelines presented in this guide to help you purchase a specific computer, along with software, peripherals, and other accessories.

Many of the desktop computer guidelines presented also apply to the purchase of a notebook computer and a Tablet PC. Later in this guide, sections on purchasing a notebook computer or Tablet PC address additional considerations specific to those computer types.

This guide concentrates on recommendations for purchasing a desktop computer or mobile computer.

HOW TO PURCHASE A DESKTOP COMPUTER

Once you have decided that a desktop computer is most suited to your computing needs, the next step is to determine specific software, hardware, peripheral devices, and services to purchase, as well as where to buy the computer.

1 Determine the specific software you want to use on your computer.
Before deciding to purchase software, be sure it contains the features necessary for the tasks you want to perform. Rely on the computer users in whom you have confidence to help you decide on the software to use. The minimum requirements of the software you select may determine the operating system (Microsoft Windows Vista, Linux, UNIX, Mac OS X) you need. If you have decided to use a particular operating system that does not support software you want to use, you may be able to purchase similar software from other manufacturers.

Many Web sites and trade magazines, such as those listed in Figure 38 on the next page, provide reviews of software products. These Web sites frequently have articles that rate computers and software on cost, performance, and support.

Your hardware requirements depend on the minimum requirements of the software you will run on your computer.

Some software requires more memory and disk space than others, as well as additional input, output, and storage devices. For example, suppose you want to run software that can copy one CD's or DVD's contents directly to another CD or DVD, without first copying the data to your hard disk. To support that, you should consider a desktop computer or a high-end notebook computer, because the computer will need two CD or DVD drives: one that reads from a CD or DVD, and one that reads from and writes on a CD or DVD. If you plan to run software that allows your computer to work as an entertainment system, then you will need a CD or DVD drive, quality speakers, and an upgraded sound card.

Type of Computer	Web Site	Web Address
PC	CNET Shopper	shopper.cnet.com
	PC World Magazine	pcworld.com
	BYTE Magazine	byte.com
	PC Magazine	pcmag.com
	Yahoo! Computers	computers.yahoo.com
	MSN Shopping	shopping.msn.com
	Dave's Guide to Buying a Home Computer	css.msu.edu/PC-Guide
Mac	Macworld Magazine	macworld.com
	Apple	apple.com
	Switch to Mac Campaign	apple.com/switch

For an updated list of hardware and software reviews and their Web site addresses, visit scsite.com/ic7/buyers.

FIGURE 38   Hardware and software reviews.

② Know the System Requirements of the Operating System.

After deciding what software you want to run on your new computer, you need to determine the operating system you want to use. If, however, you purchase a new computer, chances are it will have the latest version of your preferred operating system (Windows Vista, Linux, UNIX, Mac OS X). Figure 39 lists the minimum computer requirements of Windows Vista versions.

Windows Vista Versions	Minimum Computer Requirements
Windows Vista Home Basic	• 800 MHz processor • 512 MB of RAM • DirectX 9 capable graphics processor
Windows Vista Home Premium **Windows Vista Ultimate** **Windows Vista Business** **Windows Vista Enterprise**	• 1 GHz processor • 1 GB of RAM • DirectX 9 capable graphics Windows Vista Enterprise • 40 GB of hard disk capacity (15 GB free space) • DVD-ROM drive • Audio output capability • Internet access capability

FIGURE 39   Hardware requirements for Windows Vista.

③ Look for bundled software.

When you purchase a computer, it may come bundled with software. Some sellers even let you choose which software you want. Remember, however, that bundled software has value only if you would have purchased the software even if it had not come with the computer. At the very least, you probably will want word processing software and a browser to access the Internet. If you need additional applications, such as a spreadsheet, a database, or presentation graphics, consider purchasing Microsoft Works, Microsoft Office, OpenOffice.org, or Sun StarOffice, which include several programs at a reduced price.

④ Avoid buying the least powerful computer available.

Once you know the application software you want to use, you then can consider the following important criteria about the computer's components: (1) processor speed, (2) size and types of memory (RAM) and storage, (3) types of input/output devices, (4) types of ports and adapter cards, and (5) types of communications devices. You also need to consider if the computer is upgradeable and to what extent you are able to upgrade. For example, all manufacturers limit the amount of memory you can add. The information in Figures 40 and 41 can help you determine what system components are best for you. Figure 40 (on COM 27 to COM 28) outlines considerations for specific hardware components. Figure 41 (on page COM 29) provides a Base Components worksheet that lists PC recommendations for each category of user discussed in this book: Home User, Small Office/Home Office User, Mobile User, Power User, and Large Business User. In the worksheet, the Home User category is divided into two groups: Application Home User and Game Home User. The Mobile User recommendations list criteria for a notebook computer, but do not include the PDA or Tablet PC options.

Computer technology changes rapidly, meaning a computer that seems powerful enough today may not serve your computing needs in a few years. In fact, studies show that many users regret not buying a more powerful computer. To avoid this, plan to buy a computer that will last you for two to three years. You can help delay obsolescence by purchasing the fastest processor, the most memory, and the largest hard disk you can afford. If you must buy a less powerful computer, be sure you can upgrade it with additional memory, components, and peripheral devices as your computer requirements grow.

⑤ Consider upgrades to the mouse, keyboard, monitor, printer, microphone, and speakers.

You use these peripheral devices to interact with your computer, so you should make sure they are up to your standards. Review the peripheral devices listed in Figure 40 on pages COM 27 to COM 28 and then visit both local computer dealers and large retail stores to test the computers on display. Ask the salesperson what input and output devices would be best for you and whether you should upgrade beyond what comes standard. Consider purchasing a wireless keyboard and wireless mouse to eliminate bothersome wires on your desktop. A few extra dollars spent on these components when you initially purchase a computer can extend its usefulness by years.

CD/DVD Drives: Most computers come with a CD-RW drive. A CD-RW drive allows you to create your own custom data CDs for data backup or data transfer purposes. It also will allow you to store and share video files, digital photos, and other large files with other people who have access to a CD-ROM drive. An even better alternative is to upgrade to a DVD±RW combination drive. It allows you to read DVDs and CDs and to write data on (burn) a DVD or CD. A DVD has a capacity of at least 4.7 GB versus the 650 MB capacity of a CD. An HD DVD has a minimum capacity of 45 GB.

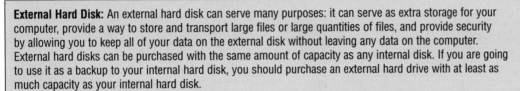

Card Reader/Writer: A card reader/writer is useful for transferring data directly to and from a removable flash memory card, such as the ones used in your camera or audio player. Make sure the card reader/writer can read from and write on the flash memory cards that you use.

Digital Camera: Consider an inexpensive point-and-shoot digital camera. They are small enough to carry around, usually operate automatically in terms of lighting and focus, and contain storage cards for storing photographs. A 5-megapixel camera with a 512 MB storage card is fine for creating images for use on the Web or to send via e-mail.

Digital Video Capture Device: A digital video capture device allows you to connect your computer to a camcorder or VCR and record, edit, manage, and then write video back on a VCR tape, a CD, or a DVD. To create quality video (true 30 frames per second, full-sized TV), the digital video capture device should have a USB 2.0 or FireWire port. You also will need sufficient storage: an hour of data on a VCR tape takes up about 5 GB of disk storage.

External Hard Disk: An external hard disk can serve many purposes: it can serve as extra storage for your computer, provide a way to store and transport large files or large quantities of files, and provide security by allowing you to keep all of your data on the external disk without leaving any data on the computer. External hard disks can be purchased with the same amount of capacity as any internal disk. If you are going to use it as a backup to your internal hard disk, you should purchase an external hard drive with at least as much capacity as your internal hard disk.

Hard Disk: It is recommended that you buy a computer with 60 to 80 GB if your primary interests are browsing the Web and using e-mail and Office suite-type applications; 80 to 100 GB if you also want to edit digital photographs; 100 to 200 GB if you plan to edit digital video or manipulate large audio files even occasionally; and 200 to 500 GB if you will edit digital video, movies, or photography often; store audio files and music; or consider yourself to be a power user. It also is recommended that you use Serial ATA (SATA) as opposed to Parallel ATA (PATA). SATA has many advantages over PATA, including support for Plug and Play devices.

Joystick/Wheel: If you use your computer to play games, then you will want to purchase a joystick or a wheel. These devices, especially the more expensive ones, provide for realistic game play with force feedback, programmable buttons, and specialized levers and wheels.

Keyboard: The keyboard is one of the more important devices used to communicate with the computer. For this reason, make sure the keyboard you purchase has 101 to 105 keys, is comfortable and easy to use, and has a USB connection. A wireless keyboard should be considered, especially if you have a small desk area.

Microphone: If you plan to record audio or use speech recognition to enter text and commands, then purchase a close-talk headset with gain adjustment support.

Modem: Most computers come with a modem so that you can use your telephone line to access the Internet. Some modems also have fax capabilities. Your modem should be rated at 56 Kbps.

Monitor: The monitor is where you will view documents, read e-mail messages, and view pictures. A minimum of a 17" screen is recommended, but if you are planning to use your computer for graphic design or game playing, then you may want to purchase a 19" or 21" monitor. The LCD flat panel monitor should be considered, especially if space is an issue.

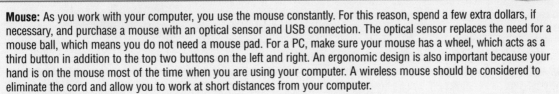

Mouse: As you work with your computer, you use the mouse constantly. For this reason, spend a few extra dollars, if necessary, and purchase a mouse with an optical sensor and USB connection. The optical sensor replaces the need for a mouse ball, which means you do not need a mouse pad. For a PC, make sure your mouse has a wheel, which acts as a third button in addition to the top two buttons on the left and right. An ergonomic design is also important because your hand is on the mouse most of the time when you are using your computer. A wireless mouse should be considered to eliminate the cord and allow you to work at short distances from your computer.

FIGURE 40 Hardware guidelines.

(continued next page)

(continued from previous page)

Ports: Depending on how you are using your computer, you may need anywhere from 4 to 10 USB 2.0 ports. USB 2.0 ports have become the connection of choice in the computer industry. They offer an easy way to connect peripheral devices such as printers, digital cameras, portable media players, etc. Many computers intended for home or professional audio/video use have built-in FireWire ports. Most personal computers come with a minimum of six USB 2.0 ports and two FireWire ports.

Port Hub Expander: If you plan to connect several peripheral devices to your computer at the same time, then you need to be concerned with the number of ports available on your computer. If your computer does not have enough ports, then you should purchase a port hub expander. A port hub expander plugs into a single FireWire port or USB port and gives several additional ports.

Printer: Your two basic printer choices are ink-jet and laser. Color ink-jet printers cost on average between $50 and $300. Laser printers cost from $200 to $2,000. In general, the cheaper the printer, the lower the resolution and speed, and the more often you are required to change the ink cartridge or toner. Laser printers print faster and with a higher quality than an ink-jet, and their toner on average costs less. If you want color, then go with a high-end ink-jet printer to ensure quality of print. Duty cycle (the number of pages you expect to print each month) also should be a determining factor. If your duty cycle is on the low end — hundreds of pages per month — then stay with a high-end ink-jet printer, rather than purchasing a laser printer. If you plan to print photographs taken with a digital camera, then you should purchase a photo printer. A photo printer is a dye-sublimation printer or an ink-jet printer with higher resolution and features that allow you to print quality photographs.

Processor: For a PC, an Intel Core 2 Duo processor at 2.66 GHz is more than enough processor power for application home and small office/home office users. Game home, large business, and power users should upgrade to faster processors.

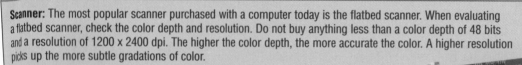

RAM: RAM plays a vital role in the speed of your computer. Make sure the computer you purchase has at least 512 MB of RAM. If you have extra money to invest in your computer, then consider increasing the RAM to 1 GB or more. The extra money for RAM will be well spent.

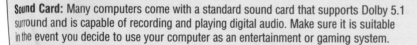

Scanner: The most popular scanner purchased with a computer today is the flatbed scanner. When evaluating a flatbed scanner, check the color depth and resolution. Do not buy anything less than a color depth of 48 bits and a resolution of 1200 x 2400 dpi. The higher the color depth, the more accurate the color. A higher resolution picks up the more subtle gradations of color.

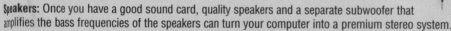

Sound Card: Many computers come with a standard sound card that supports Dolby 5.1 surround and is capable of recording and playing digital audio. Make sure it is suitable in the event you decide to use your computer as an entertainment or gaming system.

Speakers: Once you have a good sound card, quality speakers and a separate subwoofer that amplifies the bass frequencies of the speakers can turn your computer into a premium stereo system.

PC Video Camera: A PC video camera is a small camera used to capture and display live video (in some cases with sound), primarily on a Web page. You also can capture, edit, and share video and still photos. The camera sits on your monitor or desk. Recommended minimum specifications include 640 x 480 resolution, a video with a rate of 30 frames per second, and a USB 2.0 or FireWire port.

USB Flash Drive: If you work on different computers and need access to the same data and information, then this portable miniature mobile storage device is ideal. USB flash drive capacity varies from 16 MB to 4 GB.

Video Card: Most standard video cards satisfy the monitor display needs of application home and small office users. If you are a game home user or a graphic designer, you will want to upgrade to a higher quality video card. The higher refresh rates will further enhance the display of games, graphics, and movies.

Wireless LAN Access Point: A Wireless LAN Access Point allows you to network several computers, so they can share files and access the Internet through a single cable modem or DSL connection. Each device that you connect requires a wireless card. A Wireless LAN Access Point can offer a range of operations up to several hundred feet, so be sure the device has a high-powered antenna.

BASE COMPONENTS

	Application Home User	Game Home User	Small Office/Home Office User	Mobile User	Large Business User	Power User
HARDWARE						
Processor	Intel Core 2 Duo at 2.66 GHz	Intel Core 2 Duo at 2.93 GHz	Intel Core 2 Duo at 2.93 GHz	Intel Core 2 Duo at 2.33 GHz	Intel Core 2 Duo at 2.66 GHz	Intel Core 2 Extreme
RAM	512 MB	4 GB	1 GB	1 GB	1 GB	2 GB
Cache	512 KB L2	512 KB L2	512 KB L2	512 KB L2	512 KB L2	2 MB L3
Hard Disk	250 GB	300 GB	500 GB	100 GB	500 GB	1.5 TB
LCD Flat Panel	17" or 19"	21"	19" or 21"	17" Wide Display	19" of 21"	23"
Video Card	256 MB	512 MB	256 MB	256 MB	256 MB	256 MB
CD/DVD Bay 1	CD-RW	Blue-ray or HD DVD reader/writer	CD-RW	CD-RW/DVD	CD-RW	Blue-ray or HD DVD reader/writer
CD/DVD Bay 2	DVD+RW	DVD+RW	DVD+RW	DVD+RW	DVD+RW	DVD+RW
Printer	Color Ink-Jet	Color Ink-Jet	18 ppm Laser	Portable Ink-Jet	50 ppm Laser	10 ppm Color Laser
PC Video Camera	Yes	Yes	Yes	Yes	Yes	Yes
Fax/Modem	Yes	Yes	Yes	Yes	Yes	Yes
Microphone	Close-Talk Headset With Gain Adjustment	Close-Talk Headset With Gain Adjustment	Close-Talk Headset With Gain Adjustment	Close-Talk Headset With Gain Adjustment	Close-Talk Headset With Gain Adjustment	Close-Talk Headset With Gain Adjustment
Speakers	5.1 Dolby Surround	5.1 Dolby Surround	5.1 Dolby Surround	Stereo	5.1 Dolby Surround	5.1 Dolby Surround
Pointing Device	IntelliMouse or Optical Mouse	Laser Mouse and Joystick	IntelliMouse or Optical Mouse	Touchpad or Pointing Stick and Laser Mouse	IntelliMouse or Optical Mouse	IntelliMouse or Laser Mouse and Joystick
Keyboard	Yes	Yes	Yes	Built-In	Yes	Yes
Backup Disk/Tape Drive	External or Removable Hard Disk	External or Removable Hard Disk	External or Removable Hard Disk	External or Removable Hard Disk	Tape Drive	External or Removable Hard Disk
USB Flash Drive	256 MB	512 MB	512 MB	512 MB	4 GB	2 GB
Sound Card	Sound Blaster Compatible	Sound Blaster Audigy 2	Sound Blaster Compatible	Built-In	Sound Blaster Compatible	Sound Blaster Audigy 2
Network Card	Yes	Yes	Yes	Yes	Yes	Yes
TV-Out Connector	Yes	Yes	Yes	Yes	Yes	Yes
USB 2.0 Port	6	8	6	4	9	10
FireWire Port	2	2	2	1	2	2
SOFTWARE						
Operating System	Windows Vista Home Basic	Windows Vista Home Premium	Windows Vista Business	Windows Vista Business	Windows Vista Enterprise	Windows Vista Ultimate
Application Suite	Office Standard 2007	Office Standard 2007	Office Small Business 2007	Office Small Business 2007	Office Professional 2007	Office Professional 2007
Antivirus	Yes, 12-Mo. Subscription	Yes, 12-Mo. Subscription	Yes, 12-Mo. Subscription	Yes, 12-Mo. Subscription	Yes, 12-Mo. Subscription	Yes, 12-Mo. Subscription
Internet Access	Cable, DSL, or Dial-up	Cable or DSL	Cable or DSL	Wireless or Dial-up	LAN/WAN (T1/T3)	Cable or DSL
OTHER						
Surge Protector	Yes	Yes	Yes	Portable	Yes	Yes
Warranty	3-Year Limited, 1-Year Next Business Day On-Site Service	3-Year Limited, 1-Year Next Business Day On-Site Service	3-year On-Site Service	3-Year Limited, 1-Year Next Business Day On-Site Service	3-year On-Site Service	3-year On-Site Service
Other		Wheel	Postage Printer	Docking Station Carrying Case Fingerprint Scanner Portable Data Projector		Graphics Tablet Plotter or Large-Format Printer

Optional Components for all Categories	
802.11g Wireless Card	Graphics Tablet
Bluetooth Enabled	Portable Media Player
Biometric Input Device	IrDA Port
Card Reader/Writer	Multifunction Peripheral
Digital Camera	Photo Printer
Digital Video Capture Device	Port Hub Expander
Digital Video Camera	Portable Data Projector
Dual-Monitor Support with Second Monitor	Scanner
Ergonomic Keyboard	TV/FM Tuner
External Hard Disk	Uninterruptible Power Supply

FIGURE 41   Base desktop and mobile computer components and optional components. A copy of the Base Components worksheet is part of the Data Files for Students. To obtain a copy of the Data Files for Students, see the inside back cover of this book for instructions.

6 **Determine whether you want to use telephone lines or broadband (cable or DSL) to access the Internet.**

If your computer has a modem, then you can access the Internet using a standard telephone line. Ordinarily, you call a local or toll-free 800 number to connect to an ISP (see Guideline 7 on the next page). Using a dial-up Internet connection is relatively inexpensive but slow.

DSL and cable connections provide much faster Internet connections, which are ideal if you want faster file download speeds for software, digital photos, and music. As you would expect, they also are more expensive. DSL, which is available through local telephone companies, also may require that you subscribe to an ISP. Cable is available through your local cable television provider and some online service providers (OSPs). If you get cable, then you would not use a separate Internet service provider or online service provider.

7 **If you are using a dial-up or wireless connection to connect to the Internet, then select an ISP or OSP.**

You can access the Internet via telephone lines in one of two ways: an ISP or an OSP. Both provide Internet access for a monthly fee that ranges from $6 to $25. Local ISPs offer Internet access to users in a limited geographic region, through local telephone numbers. National ISPs provide access for users nationwide (including mobile users), through local and toll-free telephone numbers and cable. Because of their size, national ISPs generally offer more services and have a larger technical support staff than local ISPs. OSPs furnish Internet access as well as members-only features for users nationwide. Figure 42 lists several national ISPs and OSPs. Before you choose an ISP or OSP, compare such features as the number of access hours, monthly fees, available services (e-mail, Web page hosting, chat), and reliability.

Company	Service	Web Address
America Online	OSP	aol.com
AT&T Worldnet	ISP	www.att.net
Comcast	OSP	comcast.net
CompuServe	OSP	compuserve.com
EarthLink	ISP	earthlink.net
Juno	OSP	juno.com
NetZero	OSP	netzero.com
MSN	OSP	msn.com
Prodigy	ISP/OSP	myhome.prodigy.net

For an updated list of national ISPs and OSPs and their Web site addresses, visit scsite.com/ic7/buyers.

FIGURE 42 National ISPs and OSPs.

8 **Use a worksheet to compare computers, services, and other considerations.**

You can use a separate sheet of paper to take notes on each vendor's computer and then summarize the information on a worksheet, such as the one shown in Figure 43. You can use Figure 43 to compare prices for either a PC or a Mac. Most companies advertise a price for a base computer that includes components housed in the system unit (processor, RAM, sound card, video card), disk drives (hard disk, CD-ROM, CD-RW, DVD-ROM, and DVD6RW), a keyboard, mouse, monitor, printer, speakers, and modem. Be aware, however, that some advertisements list prices for computers with only some of these components. Monitors and printers, for example, often are not included in a base computer's price. Depending on how you plan to use the computer, you may want to invest in additional or more powerful components. When you are comparing the prices of computers, make sure you are comparing identical or similar configurations.

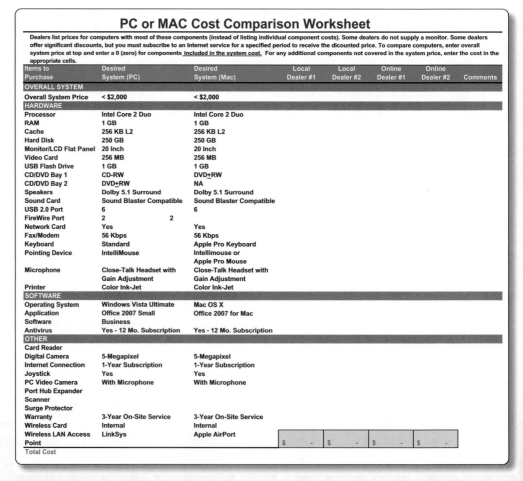

FIGURE 43 A worksheet is an effective tool for summarizing and comparing components and prices of different computer vendors. A copy of the Computer Cost Comparison Worksheet is part of the Data Files for Students. To obtain a copy of the Data Files for Students, see the inside back cover of this book for instructions.

9 **If you are buying a new computer, you have several purchasing options: buying from your school bookstore, a local computer dealer, a local large retail store, or ordering by mail via telephone or the Web.**

Each purchasing option has certain advantages. Many college bookstores, for example, sign exclusive pricing agreements with computer manufacturers and, thus, can offer student discounts. Local dealers and local large retail stores, however, more easily can provide hands-on support. Mail-order companies that sell computers by telephone or online via the Web (Figure 44) often provide the lowest prices, but extend less personal service. Some major mail-order companies, however, have started to provide next-business-day, on-site services. A credit card usually is required to buy from a mail-order company. Figure 45 lists some of the more popular mail-order companies and their Web site addresses.

10 **If you are buying a used computer, stay with name brands such as Dell, Gateway, Hewlett-Packard, and Apple.**

Although brand-name equipment can cost more, most brand-name computers have longer, more comprehensive warranties, are better supported, and have more authorized centers for repair services. As with new computers, you can purchase a used computer from local computer dealers, local large retail stores, or mail order via the telephone or the Web. Classified ads and used computer sellers offer additional outlets for purchasing used computers. Figure 46 lists several major used computer brokers and their Web site addresses.

11 **If you have a computer and are upgrading to a new one, then consider selling or trading in the old one.**

If you are a replacement buyer, your older computer still may have value. If you cannot sell the computer through the classified ads, via a Web site, or to a friend, then ask if the computer dealer will buy your old computer. An increasing number of companies are taking trade-ins, but do not expect too much money for your old computer. Other companies offer free disposal of your old PC.

12 **Be aware of hidden costs.**

Before purchasing, be sure to consider any additional costs associated with buying a computer, such as an additional telephone line, a cable or DSL modem, an uninterruptible power supply (UPS), computer furniture, a USB flash drive, paper, and computer training classes you may want to take. Depending on where you buy your computer, the seller may be willing to include some or all of these in the computer purchase price.

Type of Computer	Company	Web Address
PC	CNET Shopper	shopper.cnet.com
	Hewlett-Packard	hp.com
	CompUSA	compusa.com
	TigerDirect	tigerdirect.com
	Dell	dell.com
	Gateway	gateway.com
Macintosh	Apple Computer	store.apple.com
	ClubMac	clubmac.com
	MacConnection	macconnection.com
	PC & MacExchange	macx.com

For an updated list of mail-order computer companies and their Web site addresses, visit scsite.com/ic7/buyers.

FIGURE 45 Computer mail-order companies.

Company	Web Address
Amazon.com	amazon.com
TigerDirect	tigerdirect.com
American Computer Express	americancomputerex.com
U.S. Computer Exchange	usce.org
eBay	ebay.com

For an updated list of used computer mail-order companies and their Web site addresses, visit scsite.com/ic7/buyers.

FIGURE 46 Used computer mail-order companies.

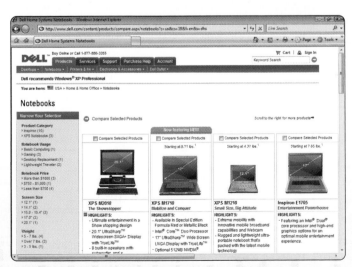

FIGURE 44 Mail-order companies, such as Dell, sell computers online.

13 Consider more than just price.

The lowest-cost computer may not be the best long-term buy. Consider such intangibles as the vendor's time in business, the vendor's regard for quality, and the vendor's reputation for support. If you need to upgrade your computer often, you may want to consider a leasing arrangement, in which you pay monthly lease fees, but can upgrade or add on to your computer as your equipment needs change. No matter what type of buyer you are, insist on a 30-day, no-questions-asked return policy on your computer.

14 Avoid restocking fees.

Some companies charge a restocking fee of 10 to 20 percent as part of their money-back return policy. In some cases, no restocking fee for hardware is applied, but it is applied for software. Ask about the existence and terms of any restocking policies before you buy.

15 Use a credit card to purchase your new computer.

Many credit cards offer purchase protection and extended warranty benefits that cover you in case of loss of or damage to purchased goods. Paying by credit card also gives you time to install and use the computer before you have to pay for it. Finally, if you are dissatisfied with the computer and are unable to reach an agreement with the seller, paying by credit card gives you certain rights regarding withholding payment until the dispute is resolved. Check your credit card terms for specific details.

15 Consider purchasing an extended warranty or service plan.

If you use your computer for business or require fast resolution to major computer problems, consider purchasing an extended warranty or a service plan through a local dealer or third-party company. Most extended warranties cover the repair and replacement of computer components beyond the standard warranty. Most service plans ensure that your technical support calls receive priority response from technicians. You also can purchase an on-site service plan that states that a technician will come to your home, work, or school within 24 hours. If your computer includes a warranty and service agreement for a year or less, think about extending the service for two or three years when you buy the computer.

CENTURY COMPUTERS
Performance Guarantee
(See reverse for terms & conditions of this contract)

Invoice #: 1984409   Effective Date: 10/12/07
Invoice Date: 10/12/07   Expiration Date: 10/12/10

Customer Name: Leon, Richard   System & Serial Numbers
Date: 10/12/07   IMB computer
Address: 1123 Roxbury   S/N: US759290C
         Sycamore, IL 60178
Day phone: (815) 555-0303
Evening Phone: (728) 555-0203

John Smith   *10/12/07*
Print Name of Century's Authorized Signature   Date

HOW TO PURCHASE A NOTEBOOK COMPUTER

If you need computing capability when you travel or to use in lectures or meetings, you may find a notebook computer to be an appropriate choice. The guidelines mentioned in the previous section also apply to the purchase of a notebook computer. The following are additional considerations unique to notebook computers.

1 Purchase a notebook computer with a sufficiently large active-matrix screen.

Active-matrix screens display high-quality color that is viewable from all angles. Less expensive, passive-matrix screens sometimes are difficult to see in low-light conditions and cannot be viewed from an angle. Notebook computers typically come with a 12.1-inch, 13.3-inch, 14.1-inch, 15.4-inch, or 17-inch display. For most users, a 14.1-inch display is satisfactory. If you intend to use your notebook computer as a desktop computer replacement, however, you may opt for a 15.7-inch or 17-inch display. Dell offers a notebook computer with a 20.1-inch display that looks like a briefcase when closed. Notebook computers with these larger displays weigh seven to ten pounds, however, so if you travel a lot and portability is essential, you might want a lighter computer with a smaller display. The lightest notebook computers, which weigh less than 3 pounds, are equipped with a 12.1-inch display. Regardless of size, the resolution of the display should be at least 1024×768 pixels. To compare the monitor size on various notebook computers, visit the company Web sites in Figure 47.

Type of Notebook	Company	Web Address
PC	Acer	global.acer.com
	Dell	dell.com
	Fujitsu	fujitsu.com
	Gateway	gateway.com
	Hewlett-Packard	hp.com
	Lenovo	lenovo.com/us/en/
	NEC	nec.com
	Sony	sony.com
	Toshiba	toshiba.com
Mac	Apple	apple.com

For an updated list of companies and their Web site addresses, visit scsite.com/ic7/buyers.

FIGURE 47 Companies that sell notebook computers.

Experiment with different keyboards and pointing devices.

Notebook computer keyboards are far less standardized than those for desktop computers. Some notebook computers, for example, have wide wrist rests, while others have none, and keyboard layouts on notebook computers often vary. Notebook computers also use a range of pointing devices, including pointing sticks, touchpads, and trackballs. Before you purchase a notebook computer, try various types of keyboard and pointing devices to determine which is easiest for you to use. Regardless of the pointing device you select, you also may want to purchase a regular mouse to use when you are working at a desk or other large surface.

 Make sure the notebook computer you purchase has a CD and/or DVD drive.

Most notebook computers come with a CD and/or a DVD drive. Although DVD drives are slightly more expensive, they allow you to play CDs and DVD movies using your notebook computer and a headset.

 If necessary, upgrade the processor, memory, and disk storage at the time of purchase.

As with a desktop computer, upgrading your notebook computer's memory and disk storage usually is less expensive at the time of initial purchase. Some disk storage is custom designed for notebook computer manufacturers, meaning an upgrade might not be available in the future. If you are purchasing a lightweight notebook computer, then it should include at least an Intel Core Duo processor, 512 MB RAM, and 80 GB of storage.

⑤ The availability of built-in ports and a port extender on a notebook computer is important.

A notebook computer does not have a lot of room to add adapter cards. If you know the purpose for which you plan to use your notebook computer, then you can determine the ports you will need. Most notebooks come with common ports, such as a mouse port, IrDA port, serial port, parallel port, video port, a FireWire port, and multiple USB ports. If you plan to connect your notebook computer to a TV, however, then you will need a PCtoTV port. If you want to connect to networks at school or in various offices via a network cable, make sure the notebook computer you purchase has a network port. If your notebook computer does not come with a network port, then you will have to purchase an external network card that slides into an expansion slot in your notebook computer, as well as a network cable. While newer portable media players connect to a USB port, older ones require a FireWire port.

 If you plan to use your notebook computer for note-taking at school or in meetings, consider a notebook computer that converts to a Tablet PC.

Some computer manufacturers have developed convertible notebook computers that allow the screen to rotate 180 degrees on a central hinge and then fold down to cover the keyboard and become a Tablet PC (Figure 48). You then can use a stylus to enter text or drawings into the computer by writing on the screen. Some notebook computers have wide screens for better viewing and editing, and some even have a screen on top of the unit in addition to the regular screen.

FIGURE 48 The HP Compaq tc4200 Tablet PC converts to a notebook computer.

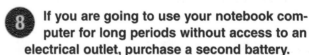 **Purchase a notebook computer with a built-in wireless network connection.**

A wireless network connection (Bluetooth, Wi-Fi a/b/g, WiMAX, etc.) can be useful when you travel or as part of a home network. Increasingly more airports, hotels, and cafes have wireless networks that allow you to connect to the Internet. Many users today are setting up wireless home networks. With a wireless home network, the desktop computer functions as the server, and your notebook computer can access the desktop computer from any location in the house to share files and hardware, such as a printer, and browse the Web. Most home wireless networks allow connections from distances of 150 to 800 feet.

⑧ If you are going to use your notebook computer for long periods without access to an electrical outlet, purchase a second battery.

The trend among notebook computer users today is power and size over battery life, and notebook computer manufacturers have picked up on this. Many notebook computer users today are willing to give up longer battery life for a larger screen, faster processor, and more storage. In addition, some manufacturers typically sell the notebook with the lowest capacity battery. For this reason, you need to be careful in choosing a notebook computer if you plan to use it without access to electrical outlets for long periods, such as an airplane flight. You also might want to purchase a second battery as a backup. If you anticipate running your notebook computer on batteries frequently, choose a computer that uses lithium-ion batteries, which last longer than nickel cadmium or nickel hydride batteries.

9 **Purchase a well-padded and well-designed carrying case.**

An amply padded carrying case will protect your notebook computer from the bumps it will receive while traveling. A well-designed carrying case will have room for accessories such as spare CDs and DVDs, a user manual, pens, and paperwork (Figure 49).

FIGURE 49 A well-designed notebook computer carrying case.

10 **If you travel overseas, obtain a set of electrical and telephone adapters.**

Different countries use different outlets for electrical and telephone connections. Several manufacturers sell sets of adapters that will work in most countries.

11 **If you plan to connect your notebook computer to a video projector, make sure the notebook computer is compatible with the video projector.**

You should check, for example, to be sure that your notebook computer will allow you to display an image on the computer screen and projection device at the same time (Figure 50). Also, ensure that your notebook computer has the ports required to connect to the video projector. You also may consider purchasing a notebook computer with a built-in video camera for videoconferencing purposes.

12 **For improved security, consider a fingerprint scanner.**

More than half a million notebook computers are stolen or lost each year. If you have critical information stored on your notebook computer, then consider purchasing one with a fingerprint scanner (Figure 51) to protect the data if your computer is stolen or lost. Fingerprint security offers a level of protection that extends well beyond the standard password protection. If your notebook computer is stolen, the odds of recovering it improve dramatically with anti-theft tracking software. Manufacturers claim recovery rates of 90 percent or more for notebook computers using their product.

FIGURE 51 Fingerprint scanner technology offers greater security than passwords.

FIGURE 50 A notebook computer connected to a video projector projects the image displayed on the screen.

HOW TO PURCHASE A TABLET PC

The Tablet PC (Figure 52) combines the mobility features of a traditional notebook computer with the simplicity of pencil and paper, because you can create and save Office-type documents by writing and drawing directly on the screen with a digital pen. Tablet PCs use the Windows Tablet Technology in Windows Vista operating system. A notebook computer and a Tablet PC have many similarities. For this reason, if you are considering purchasing a Tablet PC, review the guidelines for purchasing a notebook computer, as well as the guidelines below.

FIGURE 52   The lightweight Tablet PC, with its handwriting capabilities, is the latest addition to the family of mobile computers.

 Make sure the Tablet PC fits your mobile computing needs.

The Tablet PC is not for every mobile user. If you find yourself in need of a computer in class or you are spending more time in meetings than in your office, then the Tablet PC may be the answer. Before you invest money in a Tablet PC, however, determine the programs you plan to use on it. You should not buy a Tablet PC simply because it is an interesting type of computer. For additional information on the Tablet PC, visit the Web sites listed in Figure 53. You may have to

Company	Web Address
Fujitsu	fujitsu.com
Hewlett-Packard	hp.com
Microsoft	microsoft.com/windowsxp/tabletpc
ViewSonic	viewsonic.com

For an updated list of companies and their Web site addresses, visit scsite.com/ic7/buyers.

FIGURE 53   Companies involved with Tablet PCs and their Web sites.

use the search capabilities on the home page of the companies listed to locate information about the Tablet PC.

 Decide whether you want a convertible or pure Tablet PC.

Convertible Tablet PCs have an attached keyboard and look like a notebook computer. You rotate the screen and lay it flat against the computer for note-taking. The pure Tablet PCs are slim and lightweight, weighing less than four pounds. They have the capability of easily docking at a desktop to gain access to a large monitor, keyboard, and mouse. If you spend a lot of time attending lectures or meetings, then the pure Tablet PC is ideal. Acceptable specifications for a Tablet PC are shown in Figure 54.

TABLET PC SPECIFICATIONS

Dimensions	12" × 9" × 1.2"
Weight	Less than 5 Pounds
Processor	Pentium M Processor at 2 GHz
RAM	1 GB
Hard Disk	60 GB
Display	12.1" TFT
Digitizer	Electromagnetic Digitizer
Battery	6-Cell High Capacity Lithium-Ion
USB	3
FireWire	1
Docking Station	Grab and Go with CD-ROM, Keyboard, and Mouse
Bluetooth Port	Yes
Wireless	802.11a/b/g Card
Network Card	10/100 Ethernet
Modem	56 Kbps
Speakers	Internal
Microphone	Internal
Operating System	Windows Vista
Application Software	Office Small Business Edition
Antivirus Software	Yes – 12 Month Subscription
Warranty	1-Year Limited Warranty Parts and Labor

FIGURE 54   Tablet PC specifications.

Be sure the weight and dimensions are conducive to portability.

The weight and dimensions of the Tablet PC are important because you carry it around like a notepad. The Tablet PC you buy should weigh four pounds or less. Its dimensions should be approximately 12 inches by 9 inches by 1.2 inches.

4 **Port availability, battery life, and durability are even more important with a Tablet PC than they are with a notebook computer.**

Make sure the Tablet PC you purchase has the ports required for the applications you plan to run. As with any mobile computer, battery life is important especially if you plan to use your Tablet PC for long periods without access to an electrical outlet. A Tablet PC must be durable because if you use it the way it was designed to be used, then you will be handling it much like you handle a pad of paper.

5 **Experiment with different models of the Tablet PC to find the digital pen that works best for you.**

The key to making use of the Tablet PC is to be comfortable with its handwriting capabilities and on-screen keyboard. Not only is the digital pen used to write on the screen (Figure 55), you also use it to make gestures to complete tasks, in a manner similar to the way you use a mouse. Figure 56 compares the standard point-and-click of a mouse with the gestures made with a digital pen. Other gestures with the digital pen replicate some of the commonly used keys on a keyboard.

FIGURE 55 A Tablet PC lets you handwrite notes and draw on the screen using a digital pen.

Mouse Unit	Digital Pen
Point	Point
Click	Tap
Double-click	Double-tap
Right-click	Tap and hold
Click and drag	Drag

FIGURE 56 Standard point-and-click of a mouse compared with the gestures made with a digital pen.

6 **Check out the comfort level of handwriting in different positions.**

You should be able to handwrite on a Tablet PC with your hand resting on the screen. You also should be able to handwrite holding the Tablet PC in one hand, as well as with it sitting in your lap.

7 **Make sure the LCD display device has a resolution high enough to take advantage of Microsoft's ClearType technologies.**

Tablet PCs use a digitizer under a standard 10.4-inch motion-sensitive LCD display to make the digital ink on the screen look like real ink on paper. To ensure you get the maximum benefits from the new ClearType technology, make sure the LCD display has a resolution of 800×600 in landscape mode and a 600×800 in portrait mode.

8 **Test the built-in Tablet PC microphone and speakers.**

Although most application software, including Microsoft Office, recognizes human speech, it is important that the Tablet PC's built-in microphone operates at an acceptable level. If the microphone is not to your liking, you may want to purchase a close-talk headset with your Tablet PC. Increasingly more users are sending information as audio files, rather than relying solely on text. For this reason, you also should check the speakers on the Tablet PC to make sure they meet your standards.

9 **Consider a Tablet PC with a built-in PC video camera.**

A PC video camera adds streaming video and still photography capabilities to your Tablet PC, while still allowing you to take notes in lectures or meetings.

10 **Review the docking capabilities of the Tablet PC.**

The Tablet Technology in Windows Vista operating system supports a grab-and-go form of docking, so you can pick up and take a docked Tablet PC with you, just as you would pick up a notepad on your way to a meeting (Figure 57).

11 **Wireless access to the Internet and your e-mail is essential with a Tablet PC.**

Make sure the Tablet PC has wireless networking (Bluetooth, Wi-Fi a/b/g, WiMAX, etc.), so you can access the Internet and your e-mail anytime and anywhere. Your Tablet PC also should include standard network connections, such as dial-up and Ethernet connections.

FIGURE 57 A Tablet PC docked to create a desktop computer with the Tablet PC as the monitor.

12 **Review available accessories to purchase with your Tablet PC.**

Tablet PC accessories include docking stations, mouse units, keyboards, security cables, additional memory and storage, protective handgrips, screen protectors, and various types of digital pens.

HOW TO PURCHASE A PERSONAL MOBILE DEVICE

Whether you choose a PDA, smart phone, ultra personal computer, or portable media player, handheld navigation device, or handheld game console depends on where, when, and how you will use the device. If you need to stay organized and in touch when on the go, then a smart phone or ultra personal computer may be the right choice. Choose a handheld navigation device if you often need directions or information about your surroundings. If you plan to relax and play games, then a handheld game console may be right for you. Busy professionals who are on the move often carry more than one personal mobile device.

This section lists guidelines you should consider when purchasing a PDA, smart phone, ultra personal computer, portable media player, handheld navigation device, or handheld game console. You also should visit the Web sites listed in Figure 58 on the next page to gather more information about the type of personal mobile device that best suits your computing needs.

1 **Determine the programs you plan to run on your device.**

All PDAs and most smart phones can handle basic organizer-type software such as a calendar, address book, and notepad. Portable media players and handheld navigation devices usually have the fewest programs available to run on them. Ultra personal computers usually have the most number of programs available because the devices can run almost any personal computer software. The availability of other software depends on the operating system you choose. The depth and breadth of software for the Palm OS is significant, with more than 20,000 basic programs and more than 600 wireless programs. Devices that run Windows-based operating systems, such as Windows Mobile may have fewer programs available, but the operating system and application software are similar to those with which you are familiar, such as Word and Excel. When choosing a handheld game console, consider whether your favorite games are available for the device. Consider if you want extras on the device, such as the capability of playing media files.

2 **Consider how much you want to pay.**

The price of a personal mobile device can range from $100 to more than $2,000, depending on its capabilities. Some Palm OS devices are at the lower end of the cost spectrum, and ultra personal computers often are at the higher end. A PDA will be less expensive than a smart phone with a similar configuration. For the latest prices, capabilities, and accessories, visit the Web sites listed in Figure 58.

3 **Determine whether you need wireless access to the Internet and e-mail or mobile telephone capabilities with your device.**

Smart phones often give you access to e-mail and other data and Internet services. Some PDAs, smart phones, ultra personal computers, and handheld game consoles include wireless networking capability to allow you to connect to the Internet wirelessly. These wireless features and services allow users to access real-time information from anywhere to help make decisions while on the go. Most portable media players do not include the capability to access Internet services.

4 **For wireless devices, determine how and where you will use the service.**

When purchasing a wireless device, you must subscribe to a wireless service. Determine if the wireless network (carrier) you choose has service in the area where you plan to use the device. Some networks have high-speed data networks only in certain areas, such as large cities or business districts. Also, a few carriers allow you to use your device in other countries.

When purchasing a smart phone, determine if you plan to use the device more as a phone, PDA, or wireless data device. Some smart phones, such as those based on the Pocket PC Phone edition or the Palm OS, are geared more for use as a PDA and have a PDA form factor. Other smart phones, such as those based on Microsoft Smartphone or Symbian operating systems, mainly are phone devices that include robust PDA functionality. Research in Motion Blackberry-based smart phones include robust data features that are oriented to accessing e-mail and wireless data services.

5 **Make sure your device has enough memory and storage.**

Memory (RAM) is not a major issue with low-end devices with monochrome displays and basic organizer functions. Memory is a major issue, however, for high-end devices that have color displays and wireless features. Without enough memory, the performance level of your device will drop dramatically. If you plan to purchase a high-end device running the Palm OS operating system, the device should have at least 32 MB of RAM. If you plan to purchase a high-end device running the Windows Mobile operating system, the PDA should have at least 64 MB of RAM. An ultra personal computer can have 512 MB of RAM or more while a handheld navigation device may have over 2 GB of flash memory.

An ultra personal computer can have 512 MB of RAM or more while a handheld navigation device may have over 2 GB of flash memory.

Many personal mobile devices include a hard disk for storage. Portable media players, ultra personal computers, and some smart phones include hard disks to store media and other data. Consider how much media and other data you need to store on your device. The hard disk size may range from 4 GB to more than 80 GB.

6 Practice with the touch screen, handwriting recognition, and built-in keyboard before deciding on a model.

To enter data into a PDA, smart phone, and some ultra personal computers and handheld game consoles, you use a pen-like stylus to handwrite on the screen or a keyboard. The keyboard either slides out or is mounted on the front of the device. With handwriting recognition, the device translates the handwriting into a computerized font. You also can use the stylus as a pointing device to select items on the screen and enter data by tapping on an on-screen keyboard. By practicing data entry before buying a device, you can learn if one device may be easier for you to use than another. You also can buy third-party software to improve a device's handwriting recognition.

7 Decide whether you want a color display.

PDAs, ultra personal computers, some handheld navigation devices, and some handheld game consoles usually come with a color display that supports as many as 65,536 colors. Smart phones also have the option for color displays. Having a color display does result in greater on-screen detail, but it also requires more memory and uses more power. Resolution also influences the quality of the display.

8 Compare battery life.

Any mobile device is good only if it has the power required to run. For example, smart phones with monochrome screens typically have a much longer battery life than Pocket PC devices with color screens. The use of wireless networking will shorten battery time considerably. To help alleviate this problem, most devices have incorporated rechargeable batteries that can be recharged by placing the device in a cradle or connecting it to a charger.

9 Seriously consider the importance of ergonomics.

Will you put the device in your pocket, a carrying case, or wear it on your belt? How does it feel in your hand? Will you use it indoors or outdoors? Many screens are unreadable outdoors. Do you need extra ruggedness, such as would be required in construction, in a plant, or in a warehouse? A smart phone with a PDA form factor may be larger than a typical PDA. A smart phone with a phone form factor may be smaller, but have fewer capabilities.

10 Check out the accessories.

Determine which accessories you want for your personal mobile device. Accessories include carrying cases, portable mini- and full-sized keyboards, removable storage, modems, synchronization cradles and cables, car chargers, wireless communications, global positioning system modules, digital camera modules, expansion cards, dashboard mounts, replacement styli, headsets, microphones, and more.

11 Decide whether you want additional functionality.

In general, off-the-shelf Microsoft operating system-based devices have broader functionality than devices with other operating systems. For example, voice-recording capability, e-book players, and media players are standard on most Windows Mobile devices. If you are leaning towards a Palm OS device and want these additional functions, you may need to purchase additional software or expansion modules to add them later. Determine whether your employer permits devices with cameras on the premises, and if not, do not consider devices with cameras. Some handheld game consoles include the capability to access the Web. High-end handheld navigation devices may include destination information, such as information about restaurants and points of interest, an e-book reader, a media player, and currency converter.

12 Determine whether synchronization of data with other devices or personal computers is important.

Most devices include a cradle that connects to the USB or serial port on your computer so you can synchronize data on your device with your desktop or notebook computer. Increasingly more devices are Bluetooth and/or wireless networking enabled, which gives them the capability of synchronizing wirelessly. Many devices today also have an infrared port that allows you to synchronize data with any device that has a similar infrared port, including desktop and notebook computers or other personal mobile devices.

Web Site	Web Address
CNET Shopper	shopper.cnet.com
iPod	ipod.com
Palm	palm.com
Microsoft	windowsmobile.com pocketpc.com microsoft.com/smartphone
Oqo	oqo.com
MobileTechReview	pdabuyersguide.com
Nintendo	nintendo.com/channel/ds
Research in Motion	rim.com
Garmin	garmin.com
Symbian	symbian.com
Wireless Developer Network	wirelessdevnet.com
Sharp	www.myzaurus.com
For an updated list of reviews and information about personal mobile devices and their Web addresses, visit scsite.com/ic7/pda.	

FIGURE 58 Web site reviews and information about personal mobile devices.

Learn It Online

INSTRUCTIONS

To complete the Learn It Online exercises, start your browser, click the address bar, and then enter the Web address scsite.com/ic7/learn. When the Essential Introduction to Computers Learn It Online page is displayed, click the link for the exercise you want to complete and then read the instructions.

(1) Chapter Reinforcement TF, MC, and SA

A series of true/false, multiple choice, and short answer questions that test your knowledge of the chapter content.

(2) Flash Cards

An interactive learning environment where you identify key terms associated with displayed definitions.

(3) Practice Test

A series of multiple choice questions that test your knowledge of chapter content and key terms.

(4) Who Wants To Be a Computer Genius?

An interactive game that challenges your knowledge of chapter content in the style of a television quiz show.

(5) Wheel of Terms

An interactive game that challenges your knowledge of chapter key terms in the style of the television show *Wheel of Fortune.*

(6) Crossword Puzzle Challenge

A crossword puzzle that challenges your knowledge of key terms presented in the chapter.

Case Studies

1. Computers are ubiquitous. Watching television, driving a car, using a charge card, ordering fast food, and the more obvious activity of typing a term paper on a personal computer, all involve interaction with computers. Make a list of every computer you can recall that you encountered over the past week (be careful not to limit yourself just to the computers you see). Consider how each computer is used. How were the tasks the computers performed done before computers existed? Write a brief report and submit it to your instructor.

2. The Internet has had a tremendous impact on business. For some businesses, that influence has not been positive. For example, surveys suggest that as a growing number of people make their own travel plans online, travel agents are seeing fewer customers. Use the Web and/or printed media to research businesses that have been affected negatively by the Internet. What effect has the Internet had? How can the business compete with the Internet? Write a brief report and submit it to your instructor.

3. People use personal computers for many reasons – for work, for school, for entertainment, and much more. What are your main reasons for using a personal computer? With these in mind, research your ideal personal computer system using one or more local computer stores or online computer Web sites. Create a list of the hardware and software that would be included, the cost of each item, the total cost for the entire system, and your main reasons for using this computer system.

4. Today the functional lines between personal mobile devices seem blurred. Your cell phone has a digital camera; your PDA has wireless Internet access and plays digital music; and your game console plays videos. These are examples of technological convergence, a process in which separate technologies merge in single products. Write a brief report on how your favorite personal mobile device is an example of convergence, listing the various technologies that it uses.

PHOTO CREDITS

Opener: Courtesy of SanDisk Corporation, © Medioimages / Alamy, Courtesy of Intel Corporation, Courtesy of Intel Corporation, Courtesy of Advanced Micro Devices, Inc, Courtesy of Microsoft Corporation, Courtesy of Hewlett-Packard Company, Courtesy of Sony Electronics Inc, Courtesy of Acer America Corp, Courtesy of Microsoft Corporation; Figure 1 Courtesy of Hewlett-Packard Company, Courtesy of D-Link Systems, Courtesy of Logitech, Inc, Courtesy of Maxtor, Courtesy of Hewlett-Packard Company, Courtesy of Sandisk Corporation, Courtesy of SanDisk Corporation, Courtesy of Motorola, Courtesy of Sony Electronics Inc, Courtesy of Hewlett-Packard Company, © David Young-Wolff/Photo Edit; Figure 2 © Bill Aron / PhotoEdit ; Figure 4 Courtesy of Microsoft Corporation; Figure 5 Courtesy of Veo Intl, Courtesy of Socket Communications Inc, © Gustaf Brundin/istockphoto.com, Courtesy of Hewlett-Packard Company; Figure 6 © Kaluzny-Thatcher/Getty Images; Figure 7 Courtesy of Microsoft Corporation, Courtesy of Microsoft Corporation; Figure 8 © Yo/Getty Images; Figure 9 Courtesy of Intel Corporation, Courtesy of Hewlett-Packard Company, Courtesy of SMART Modular Technologies, Inc. © 2002, Courtesy of Creative Labs, Inc. Copyright © 2003 Creative Technology Ltd. (SOUND BLASTER AUDIGY 2S). All rights reserved, Courtesy of Matrox Graphics Inc; Figure 10 Courtesy of Oki Data Amercas, Inc; Figure 11 Courtesy of Hewlett-Packard Company, Courtesy of Xerox Corporation, Courtesy of Epson America, Inc; Figure 12 Courtesy of Xerox Corporation; Figure 13 Courtesy of Hewlett-Packard Company, Courtesy of NEC-Mitsubishi Electronics Display of America Inc; Figure 14 Courtesy of Acer America Corp, Image courtesy of TabletKiosk, Courtesy of Archos, Courtesy of Palm, Inc; Figure 17 Courtesy of Maxtor Corporation; Figure 18 © Masterfile (Royalty Free Div.) www.masterfile.com, Photo Courtesy of Iomega Corporation. Copyright (c) 2005 Iomega Corporation. All Rights Reserved. Zip is a registered trademark in the United States and/or other countries. Iomega, the sylized "i" logo and product images are property of Iomega Corporation in the United States and/or other countries; Figure 19 © Gary Herrington Photography; Figure 20 © 2005 Dell Inc. All Rights Reserved, Courtesy of DeLorme; Figure 21 Courtesy of Merriam-Webster Inc, Courtesy of Memorex Products, Inc, Courtesy of DeLorme; Figure 22 Courtesy of Sony Electronics Inc; Figure 23 Sam Lee/istockphoto.com, © Marianna Day Massey/ZUMA/Corbis, Courtesy of Hewlett-Packard Company, Courtesy of Hewlett-Packard Company, Scrambled/istockphoto.com; Figure 24 Courtesy of SanDisk Corporation; Figure 25 Toshiba America Information Systems, Inc; Figure 26 ITAR-TASS/Alexander Bundin /Landov; Figure 28 ©Mark Richards / Photo Edit ; Figure 33 Courtesy of Hewlett-Packard Company, Courtesy of Fujitsu Siemens Computers; Figure 37 of Hewlett-Packard Company, Courtesy of Wacom, © Darrin Klimek/Getty Images; Figure 40 Courtesy of Hewlett-Packard Company, Courtesy of SanDisk Corporation, Courtesy of Hewlett-Packard Company, Courtesy of Avid Technology, Courtesy of Seagate Technology, Courtesy of Hewlett-Packard Company, Courtesy of Logitech, Courtesy of Microsoft Corporation, Courtesy of Zoom Technologies Inc, Courtesy of ViewSonic Corporation, Courtesy of Microsoft Corporation, Courtesy of Hewlett-Packard Company, Courtesy of Intel Corporation, Courtesy of Kingston Technology, Courtesy of UMAX, Courtesy of Logitech, Courtesy of Logitech, Courtesy of SanDisk Corporation, Courtesy of 3Com Corporation, Courtesy of D-Link Corporation/D-Link Systems, Inc; Figure 48 PRNewsFoto/Mindjet LLC; Figure 49 Courtesy of Fujitsu-Siemens Computers; Figure 50 Courtesy of InFocus Corporation; Figure 51 © Digital Archive Japan / Alamy; Figure 52 © Patrick Olear / PhotoEdit; Figure 55 Courtesy of Motion Computing; Figure 57 Courtesy of Motion Computing.